ALL WEREWOLVES MUST GO!!

A COLLECTION OF WEREWOLVES FROM INKTOBER 2016

→ BY: MARIE ENGER

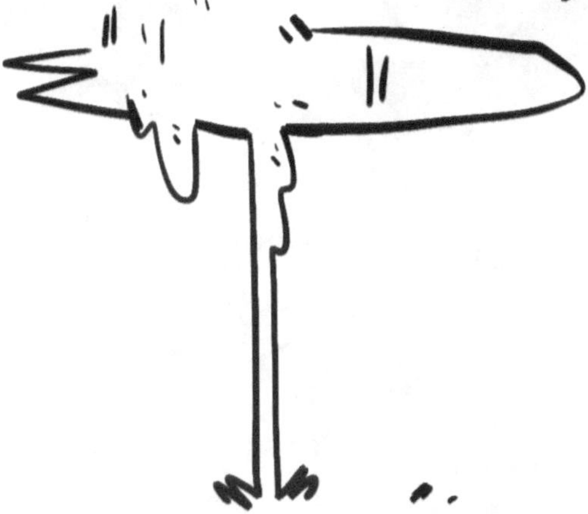

1ST PRINTING

© MARIE ENGER 2017

ISBN: 978-0-9984520-0-5

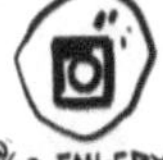
@SO_ENGERY

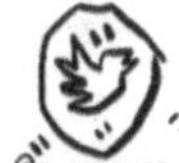
@SO_ENGERY

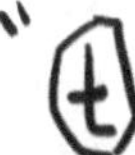
@SO_ENGERY

SO-ENGERY.COM

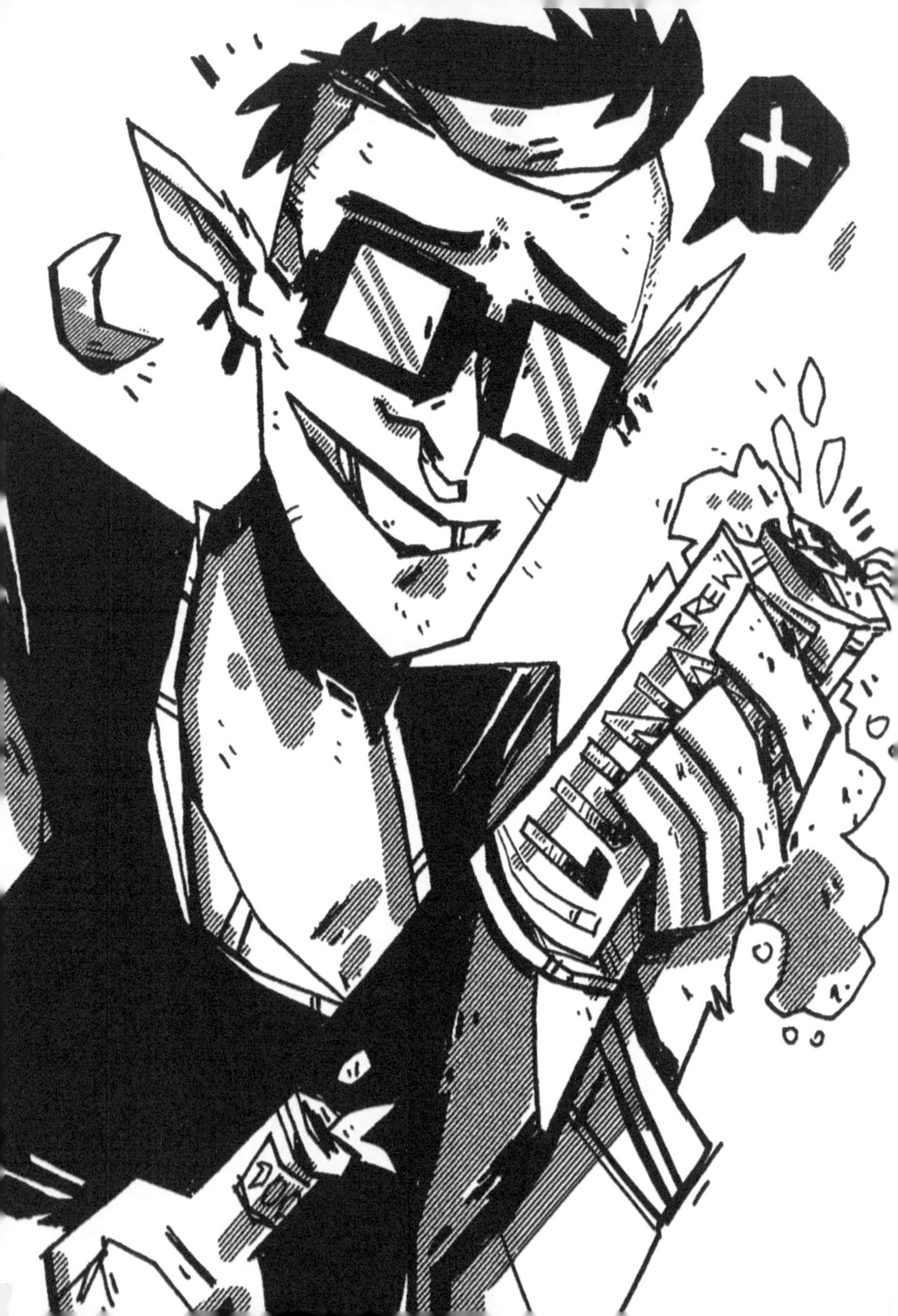

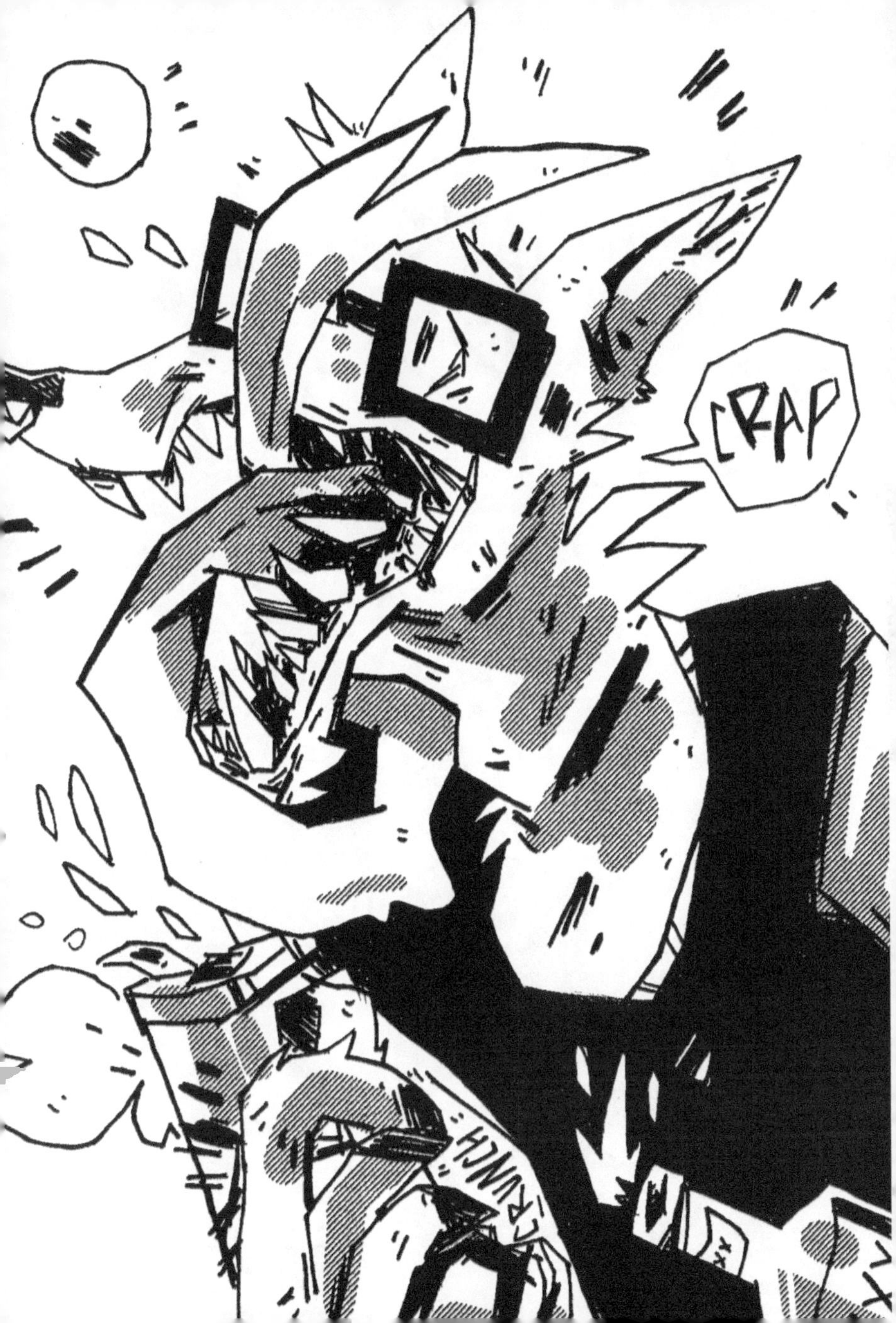

CRAP

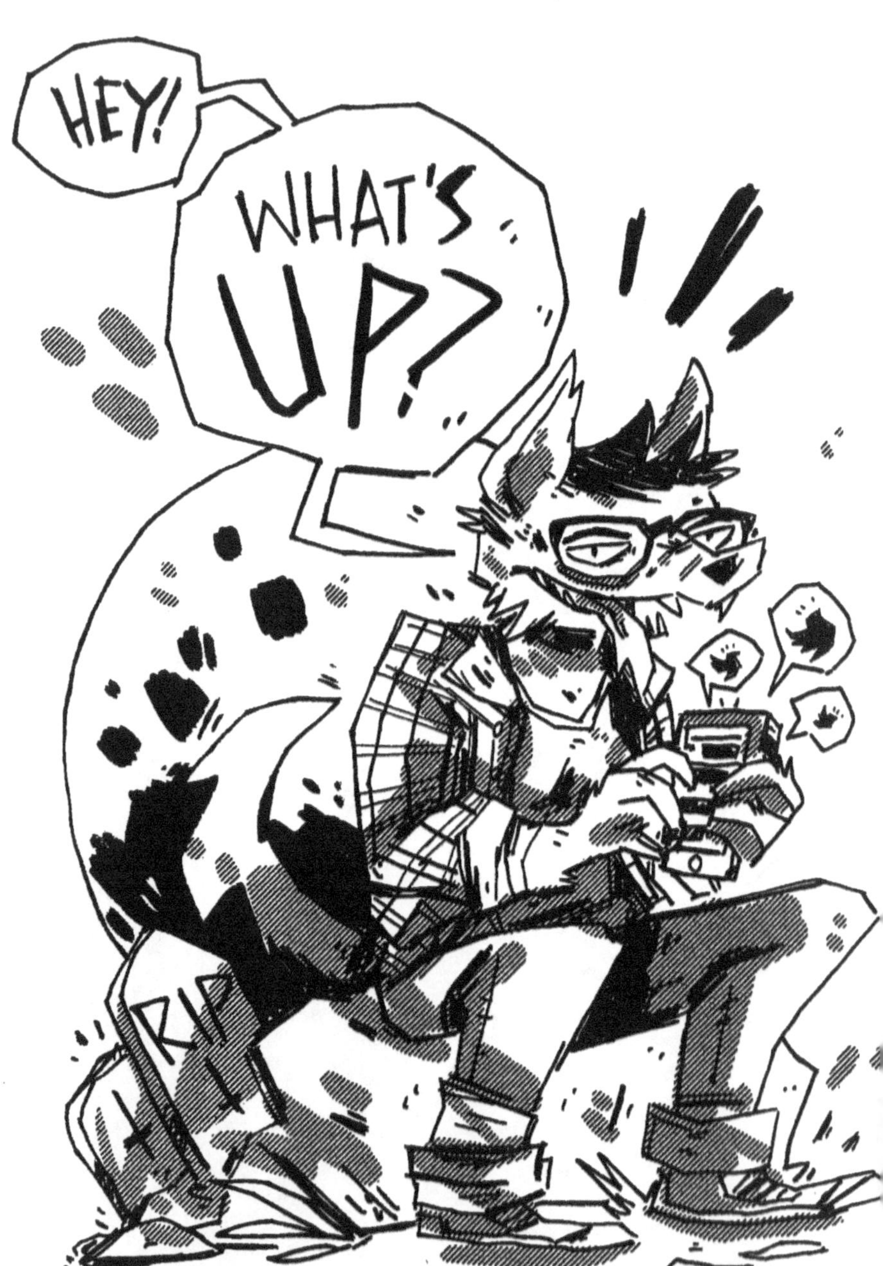

HEY!
WHAT'S UP?
RIP

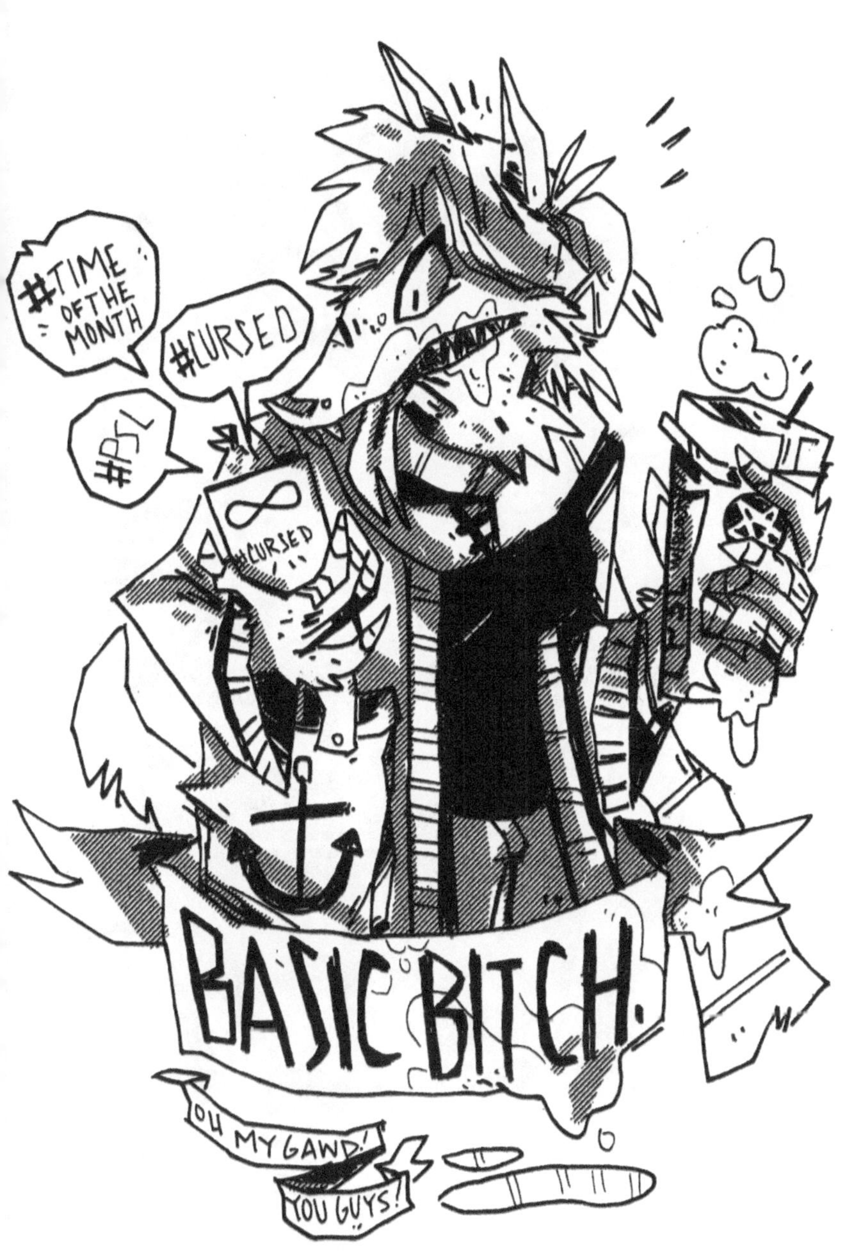

#TIME OF THE MONTH
#CURSED
#PSL
#CURSED
BASIC BITCH.
OH MY GAWD!
YOU GUYS!

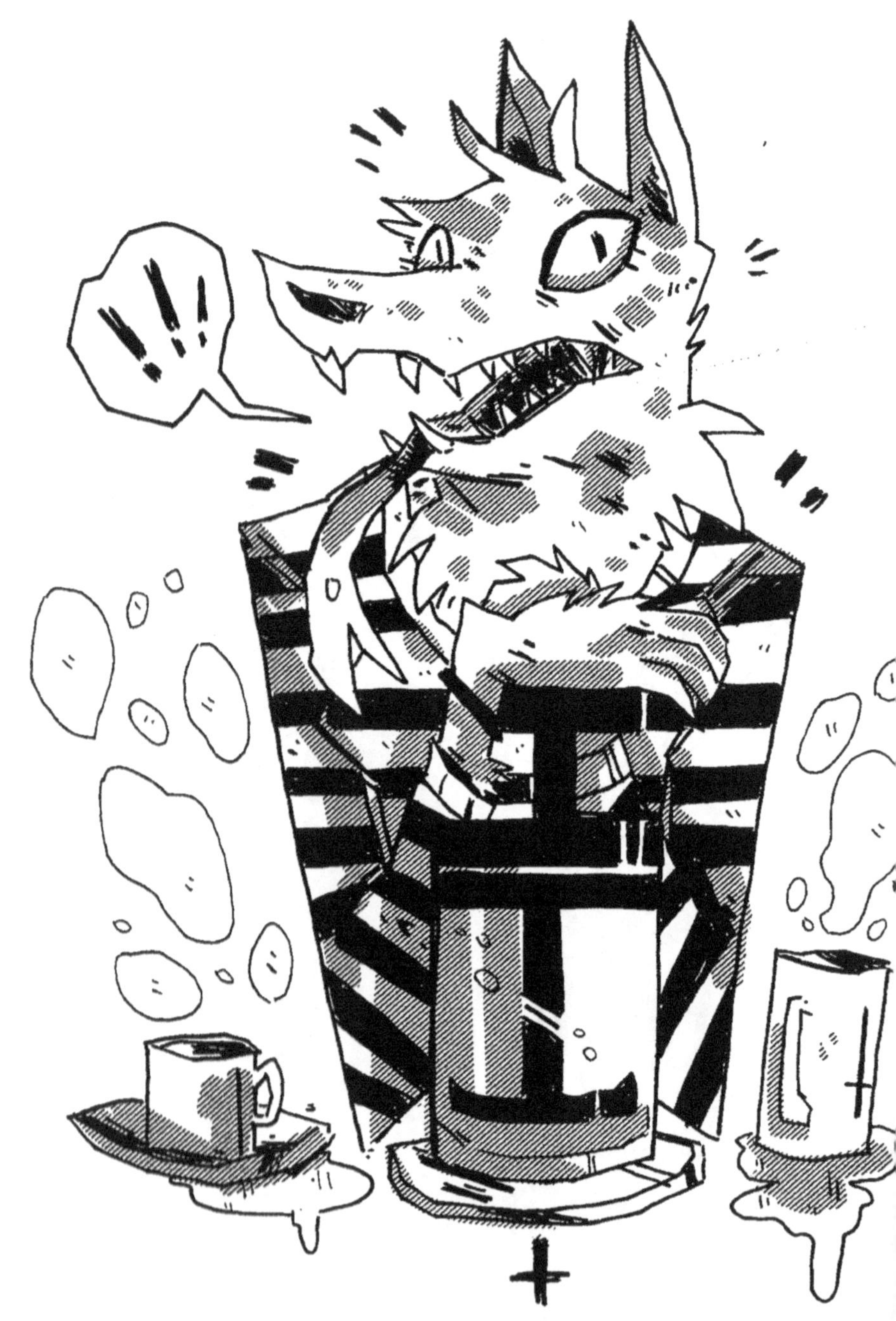

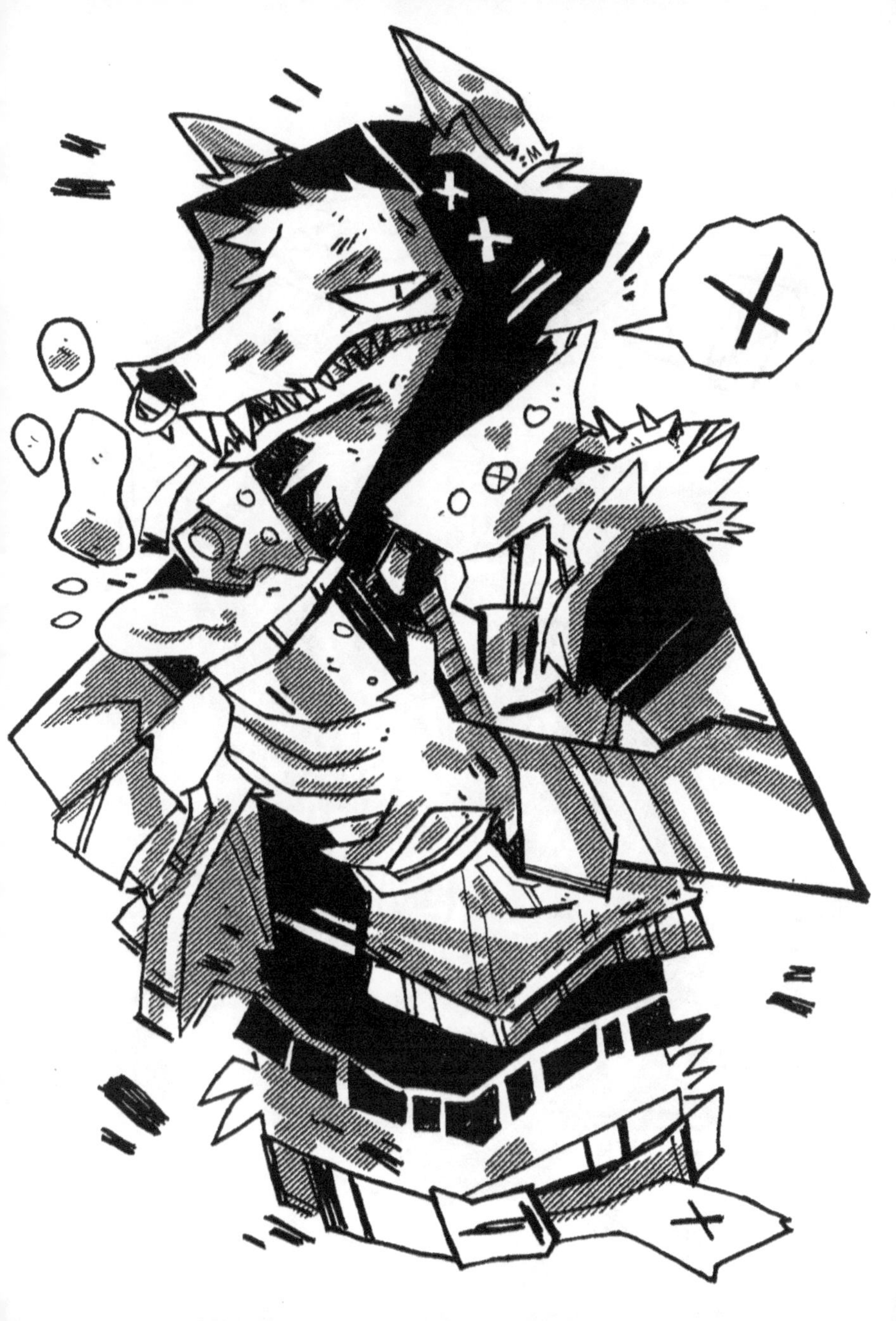

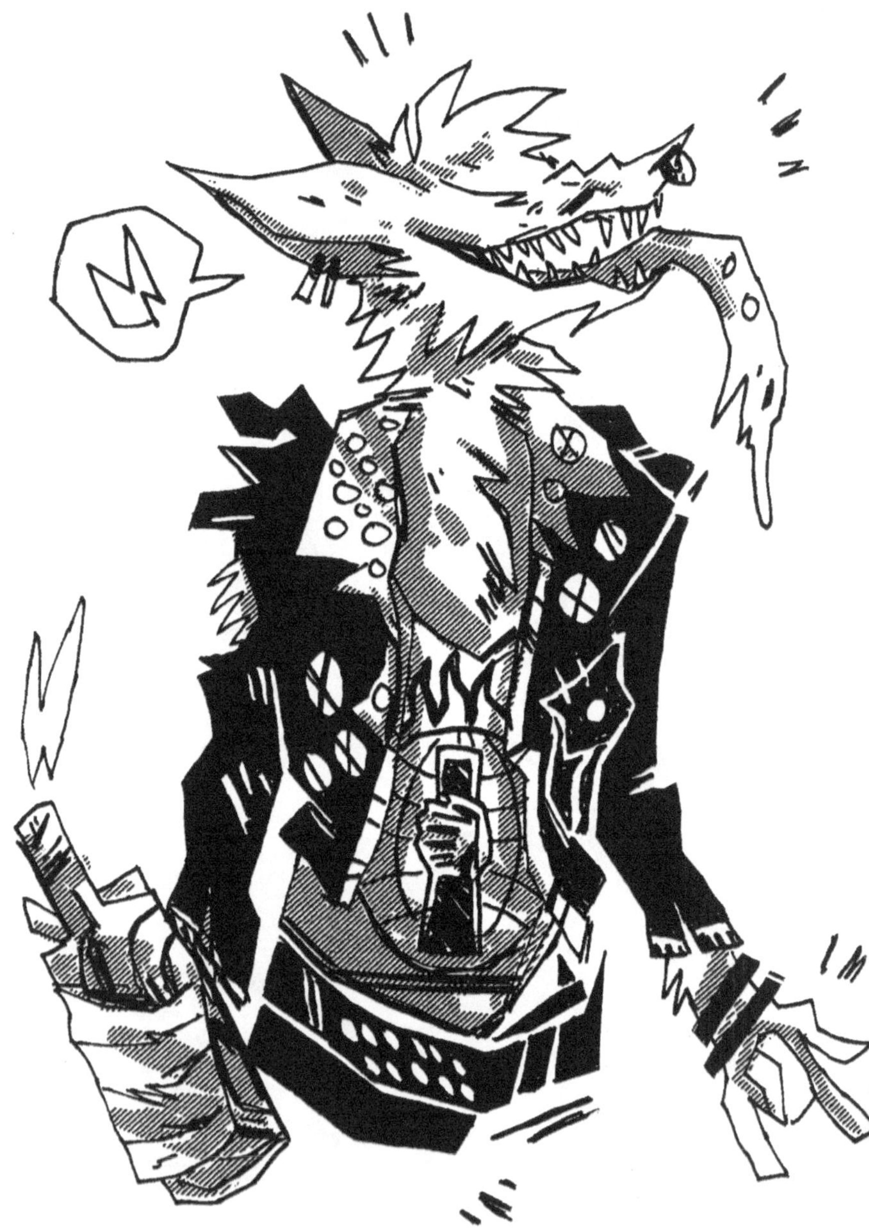

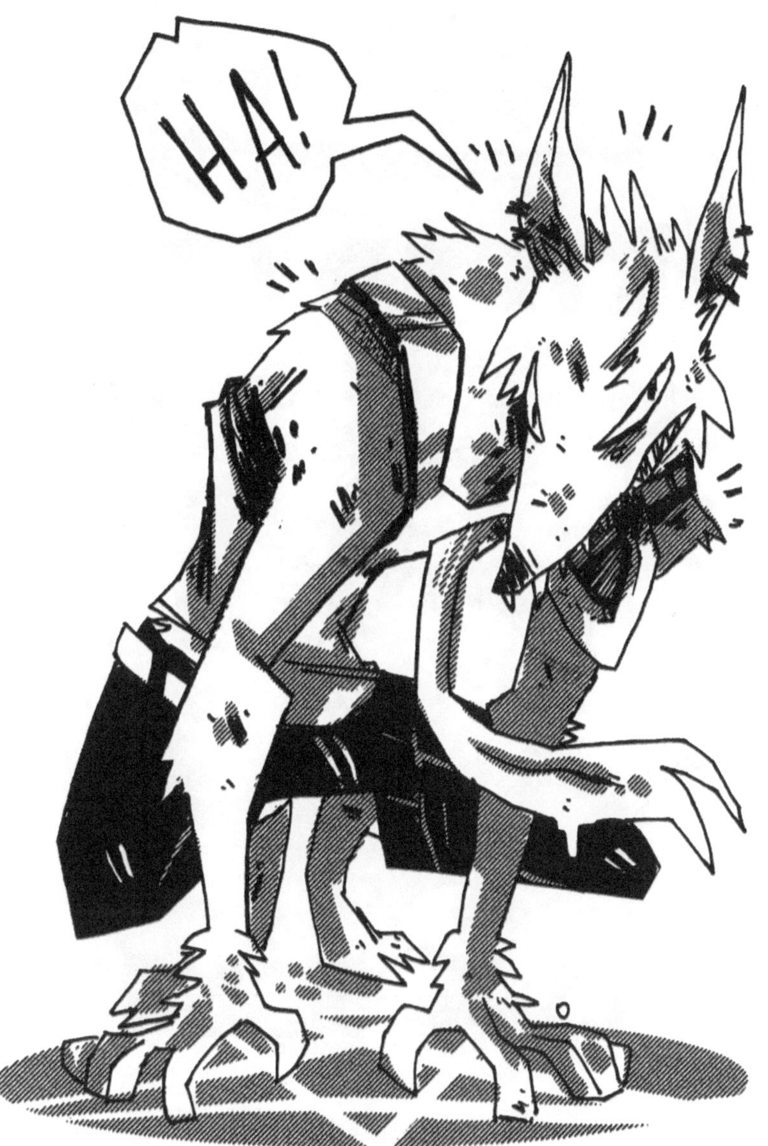
HA!

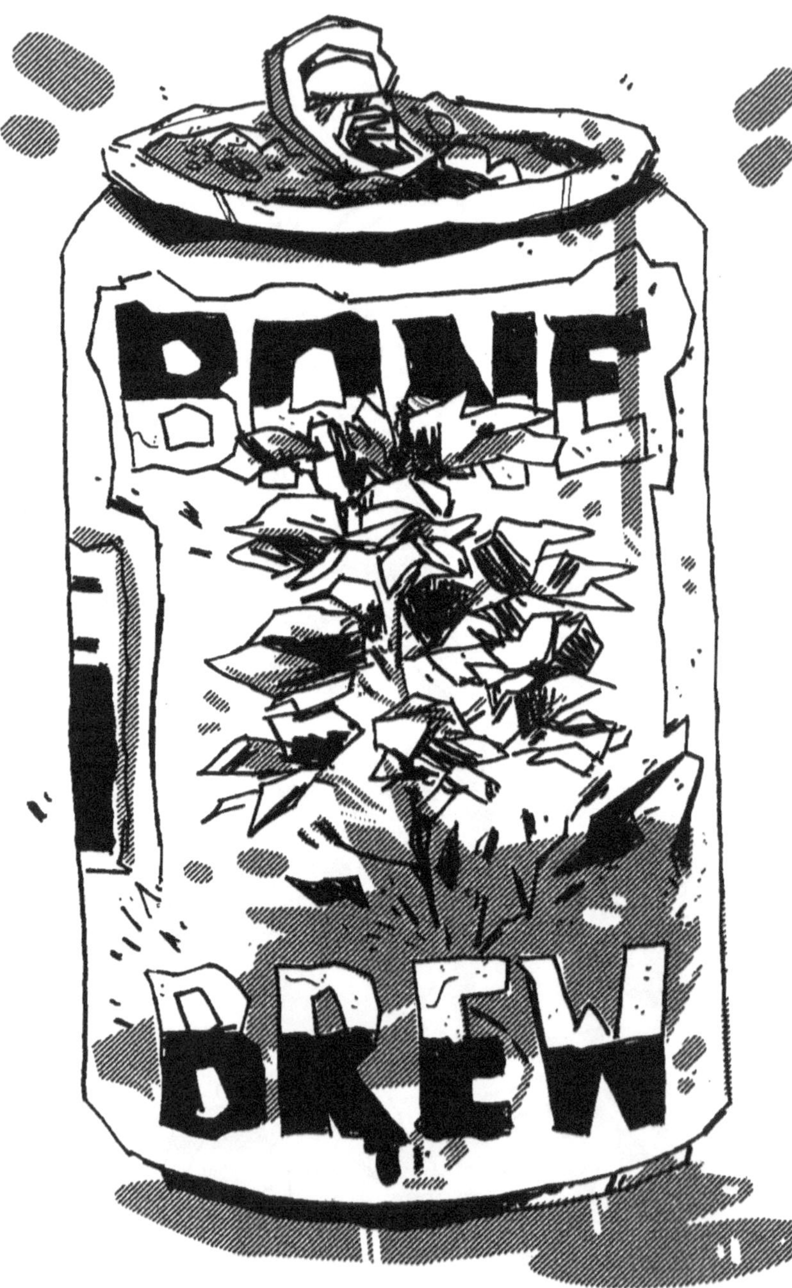

BONE
BREW

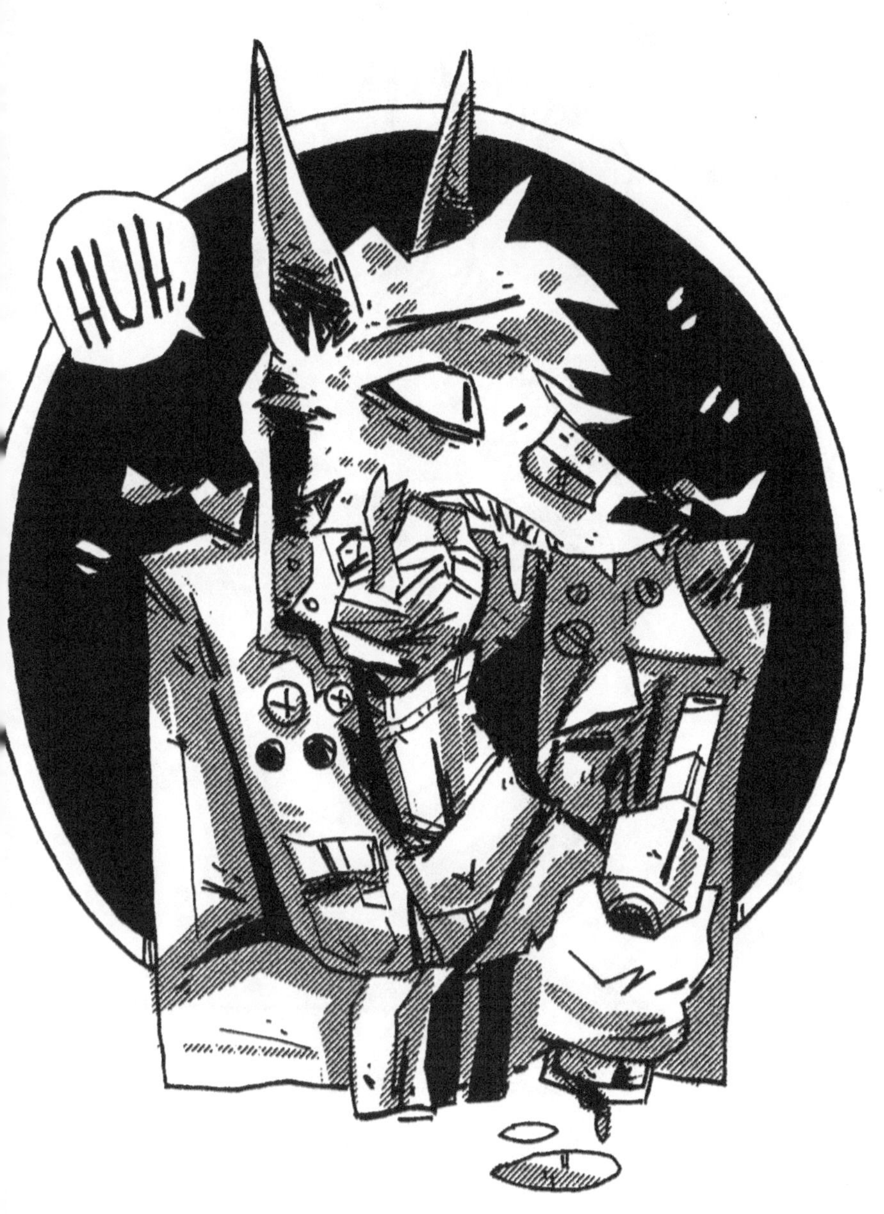
HUH.

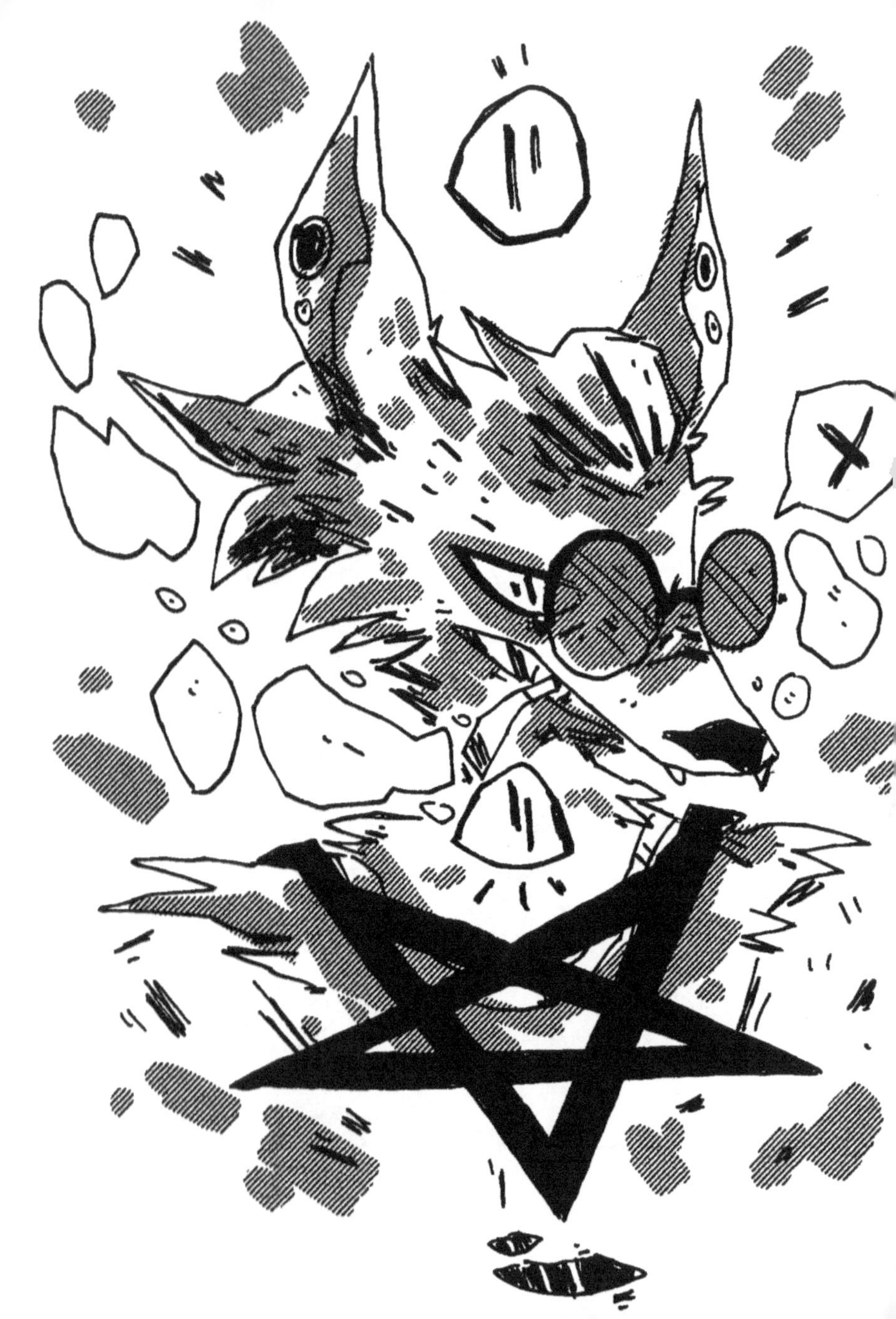

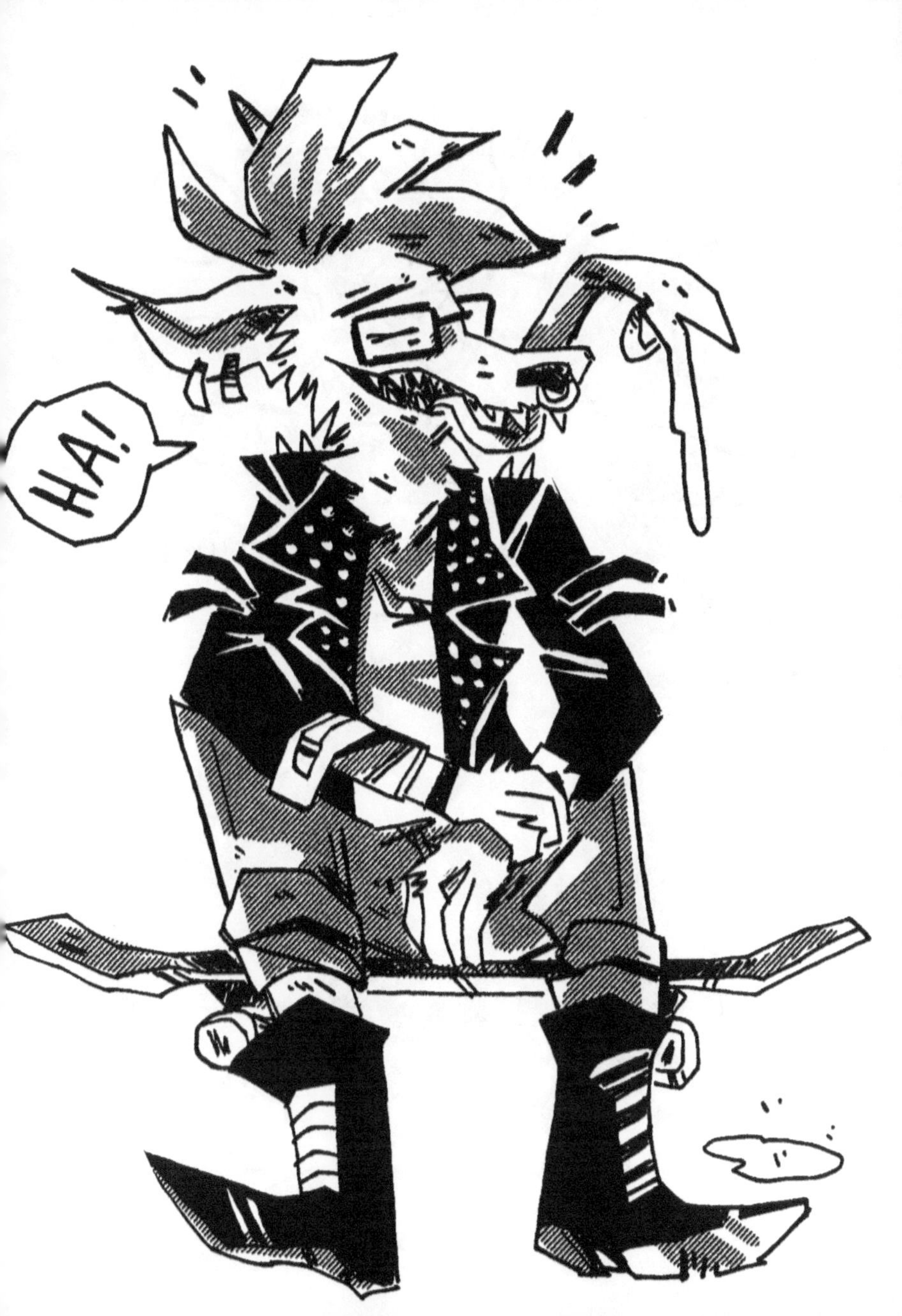
HA!

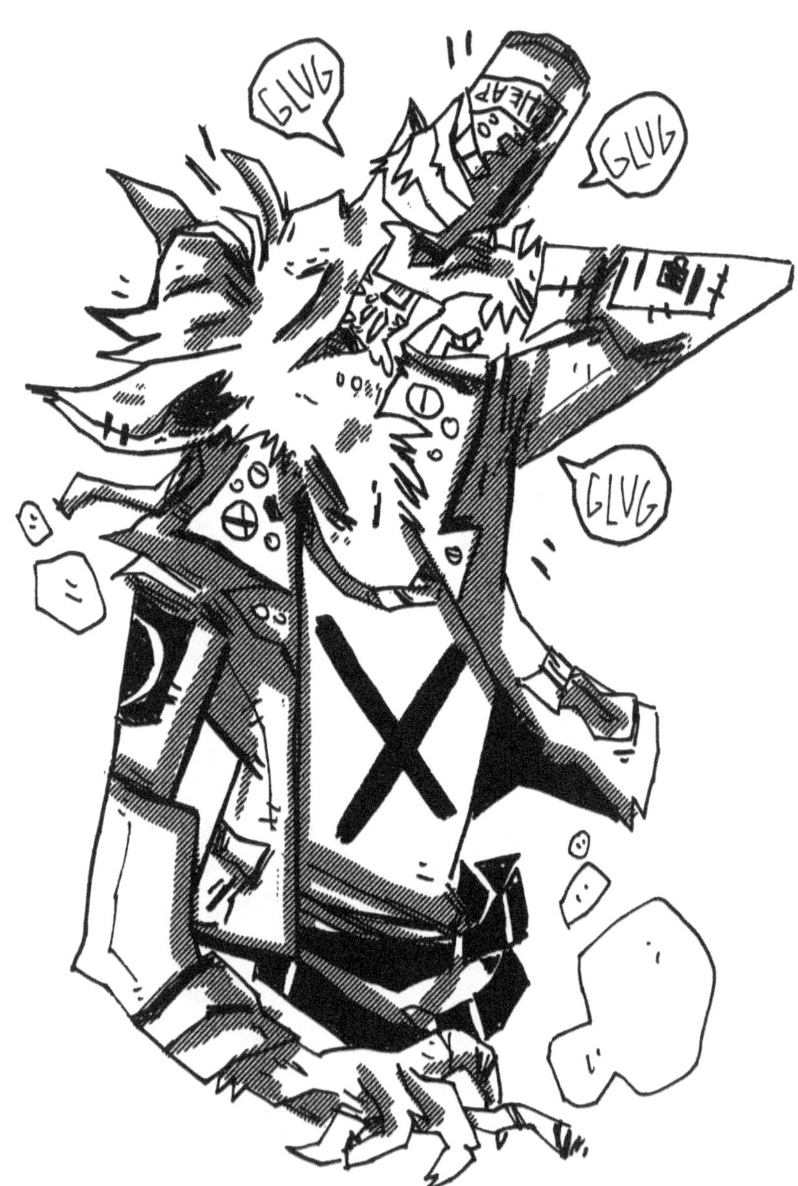

GLUG
GLUG
GLUG

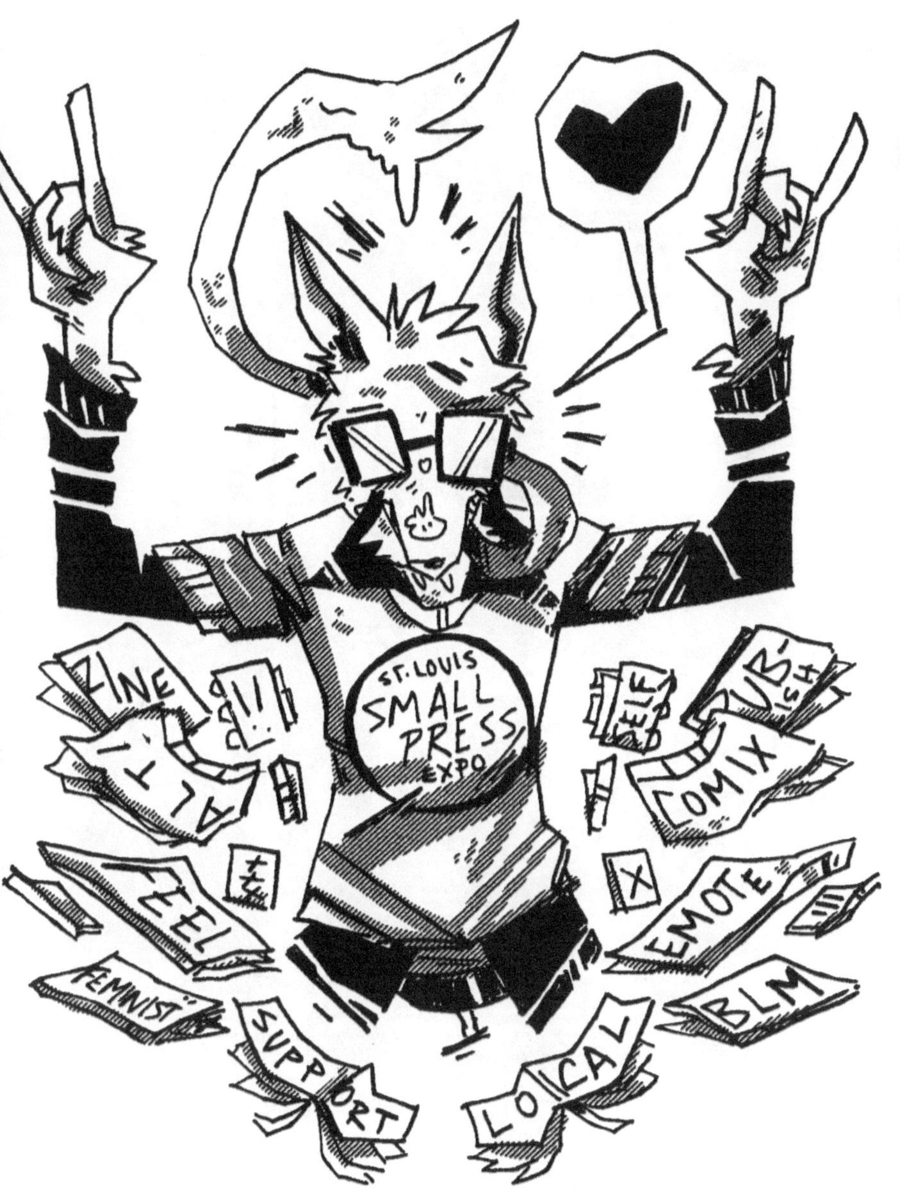

ZINE
ALT
!!!
ST. LOUIS
SMALL PRESS EXPO
SELF
PUB-ISH
COMIX
FEEL
FEMNIST
X
EMOTE
BLM
SUPPORT
LOCAL

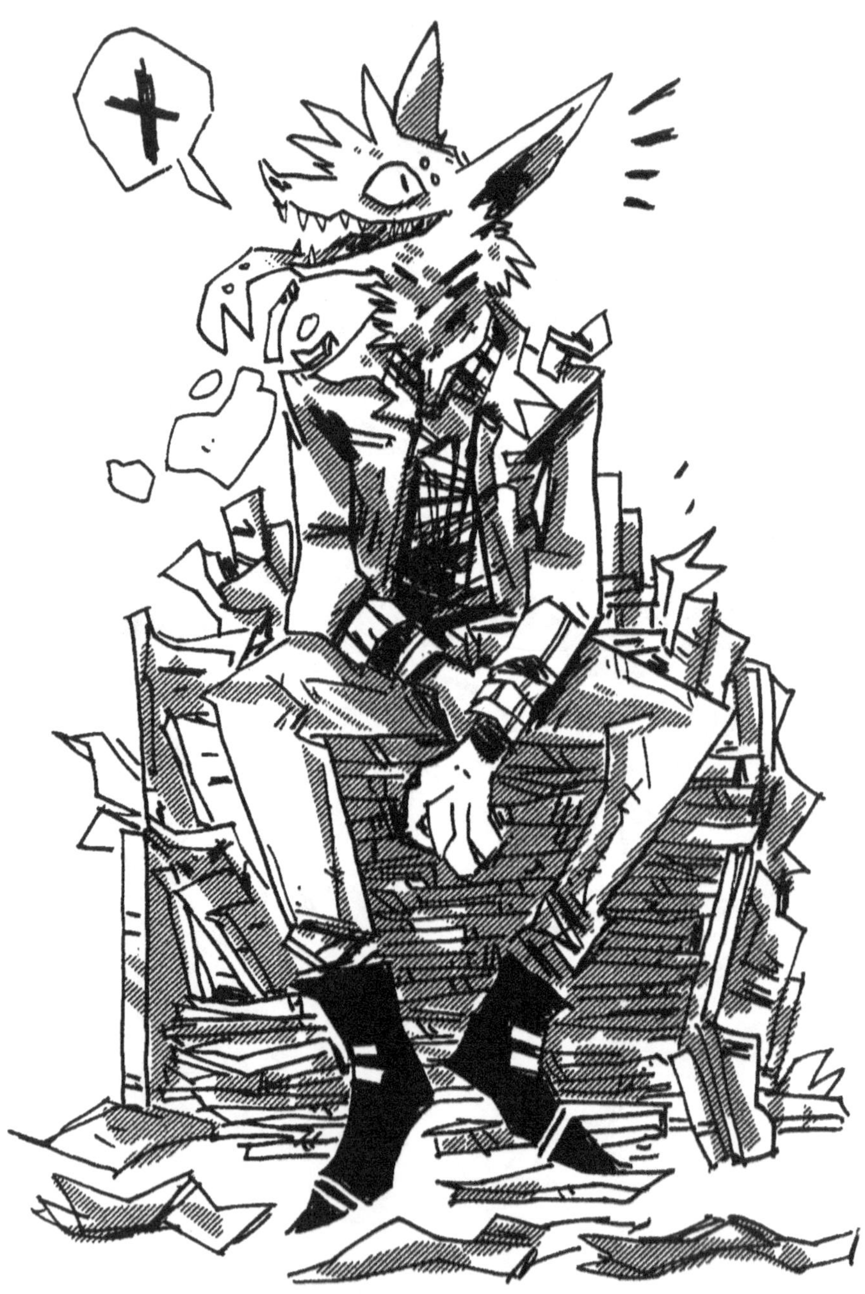

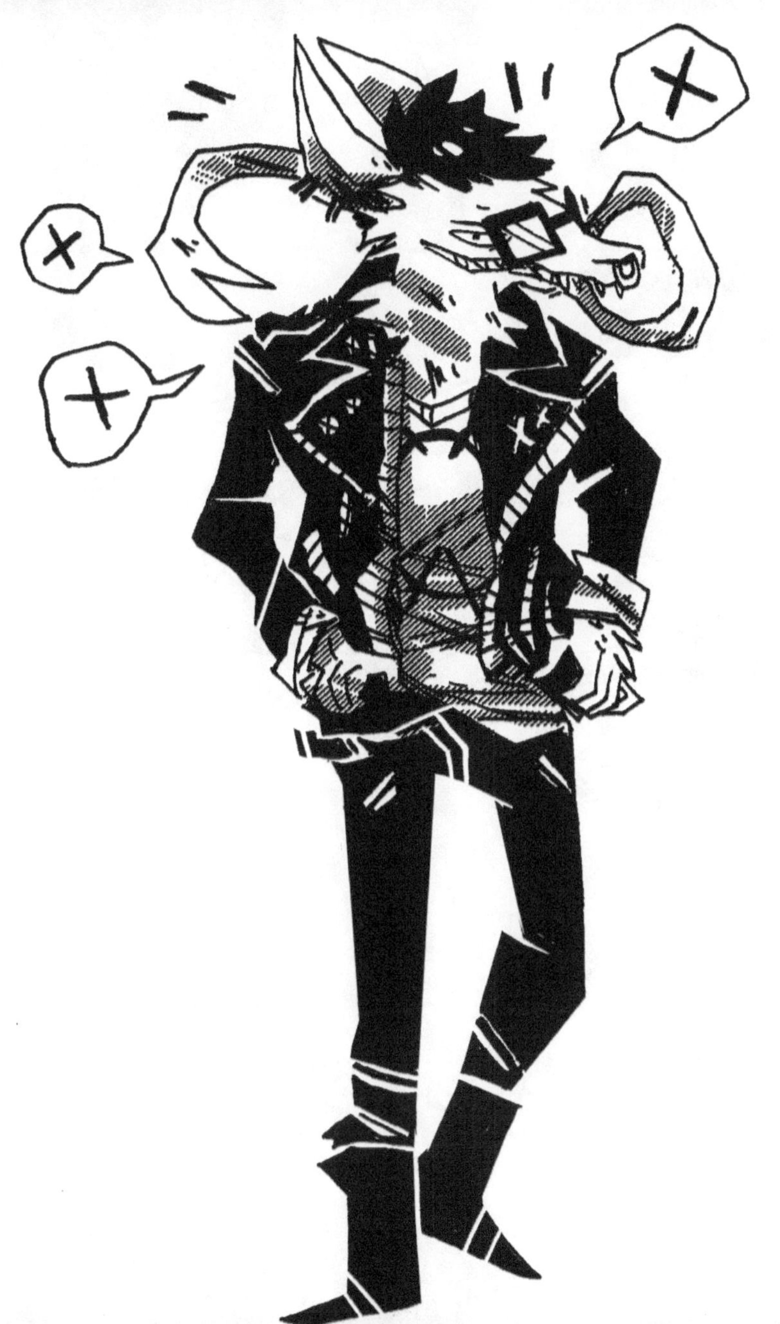
X
X
X
X
X

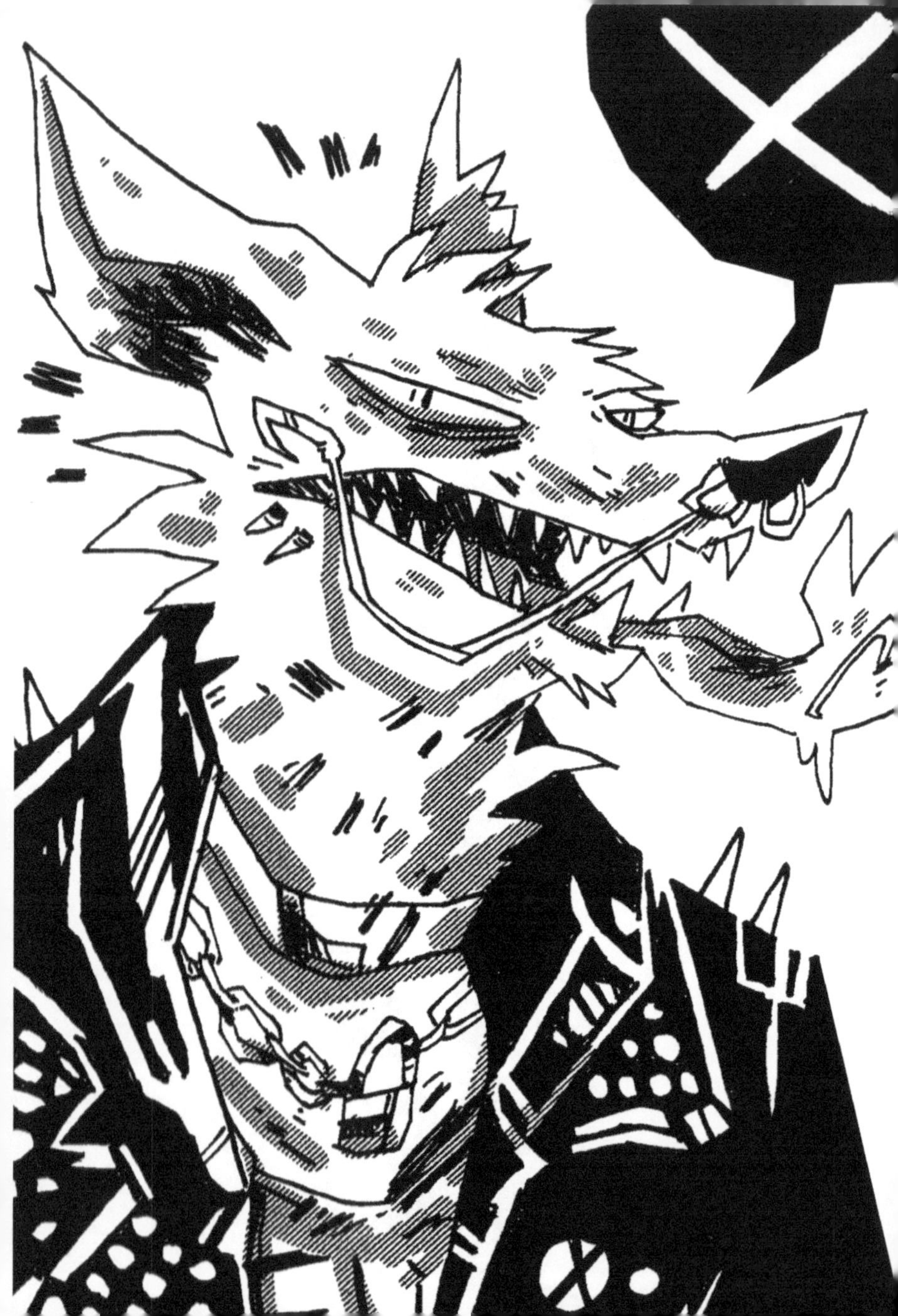

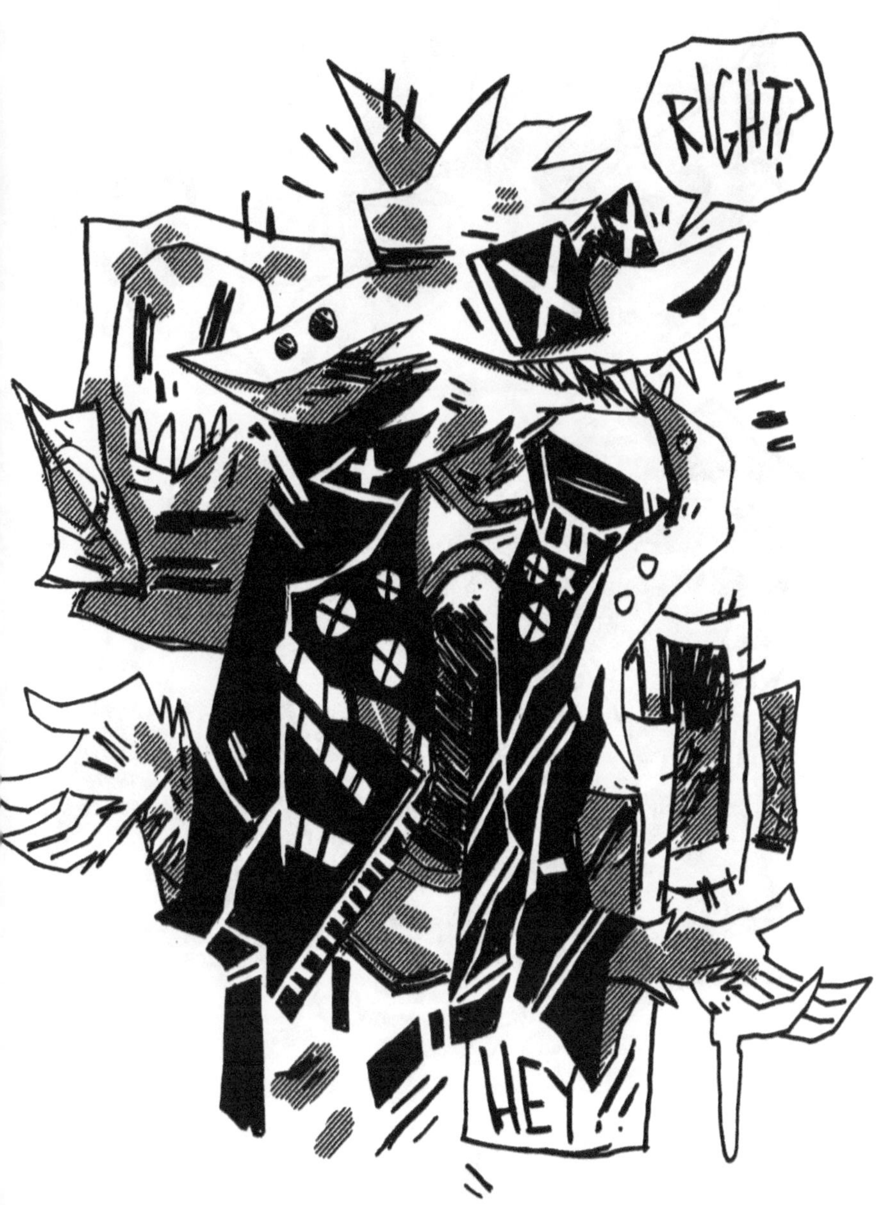

RIGHT?
HEY

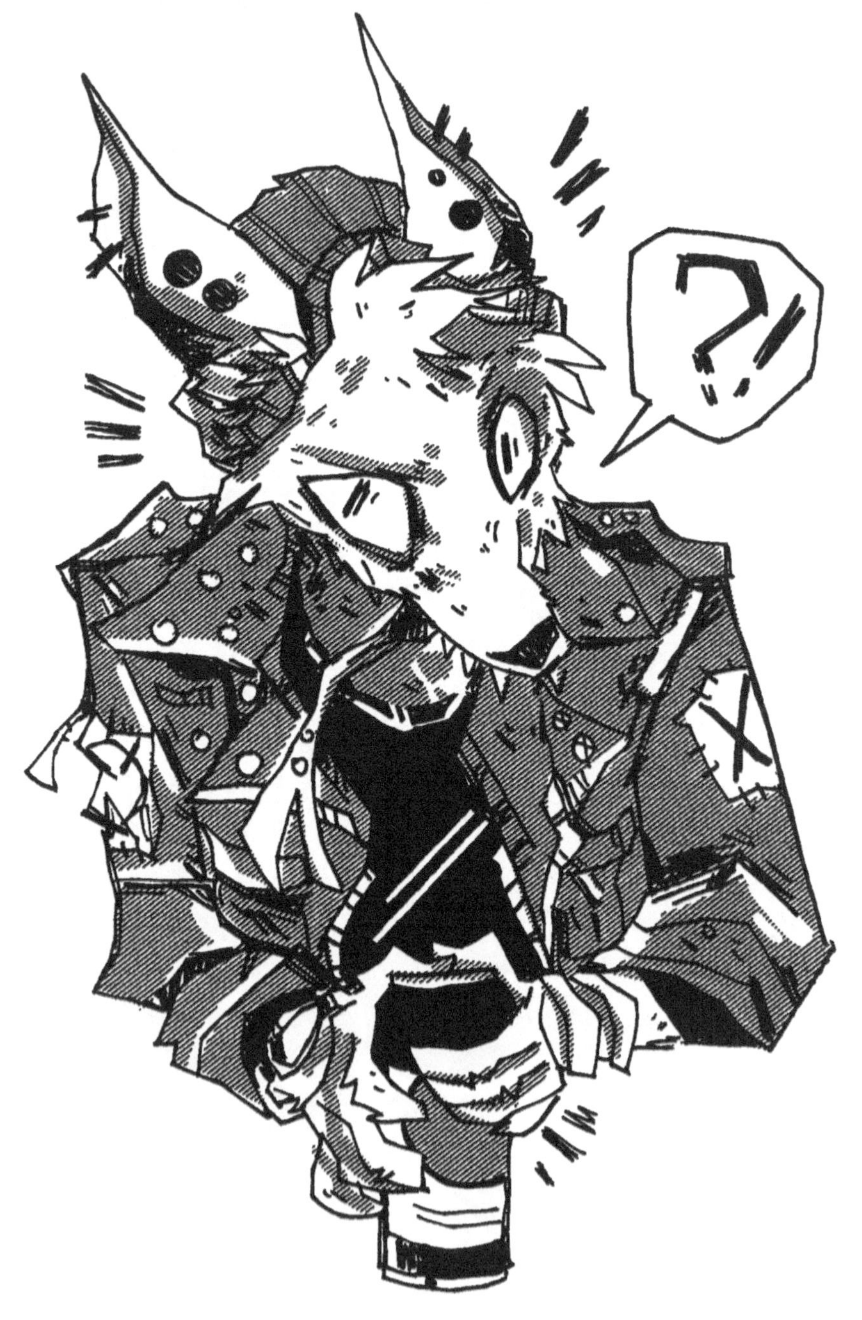

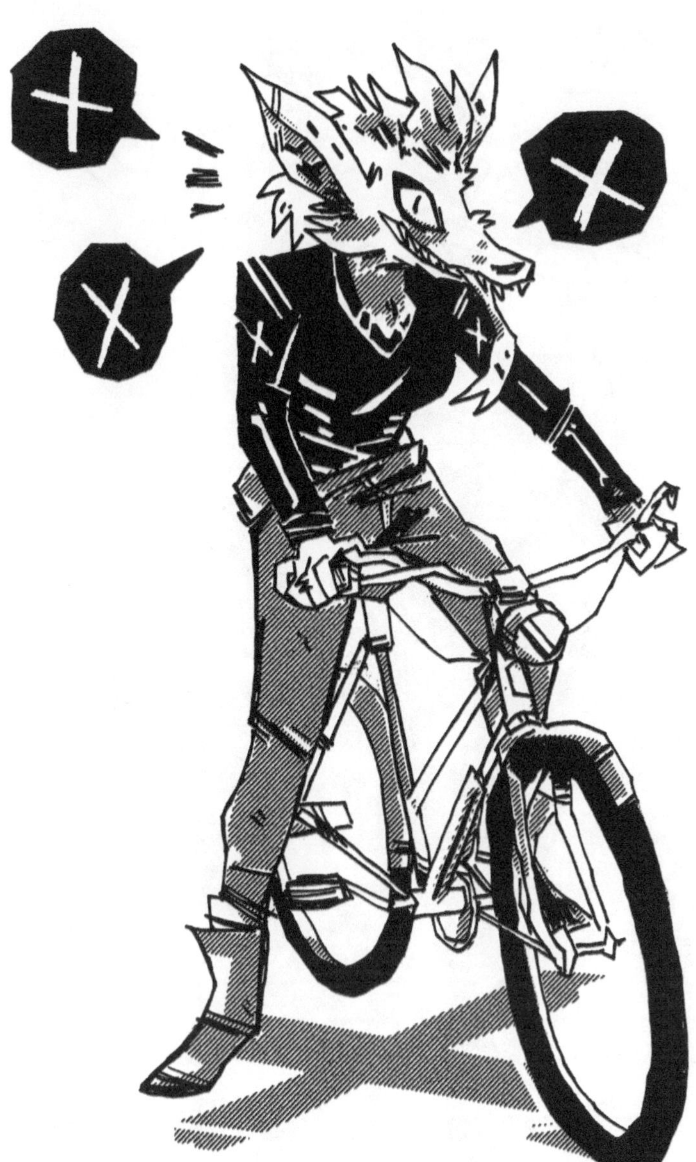
X
X
X

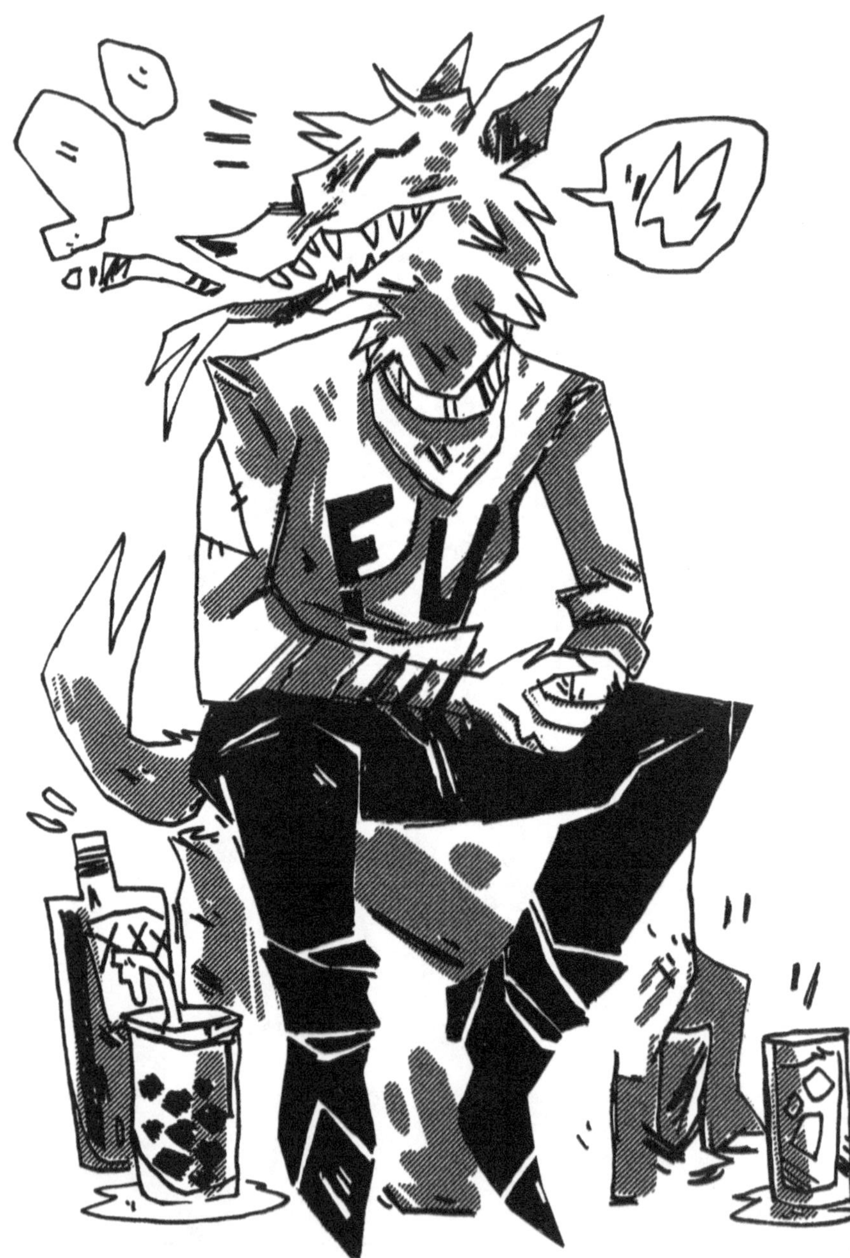
FU

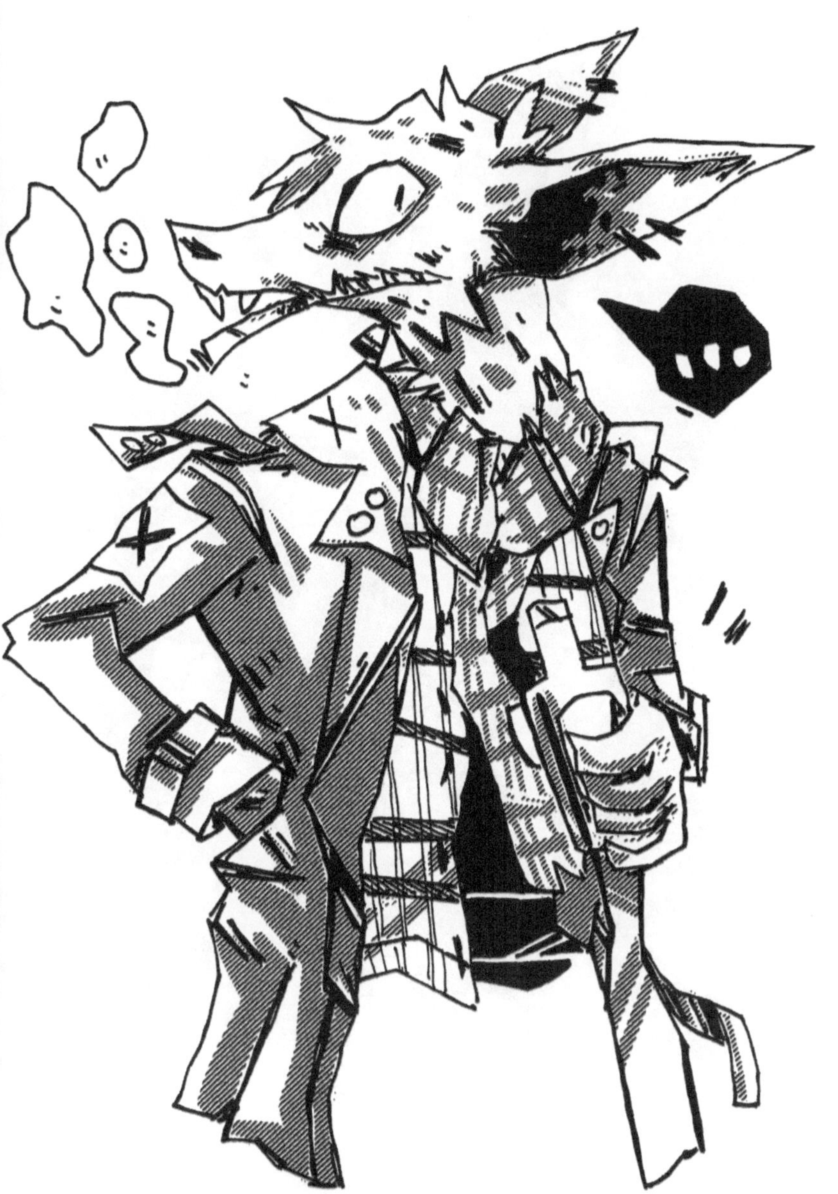

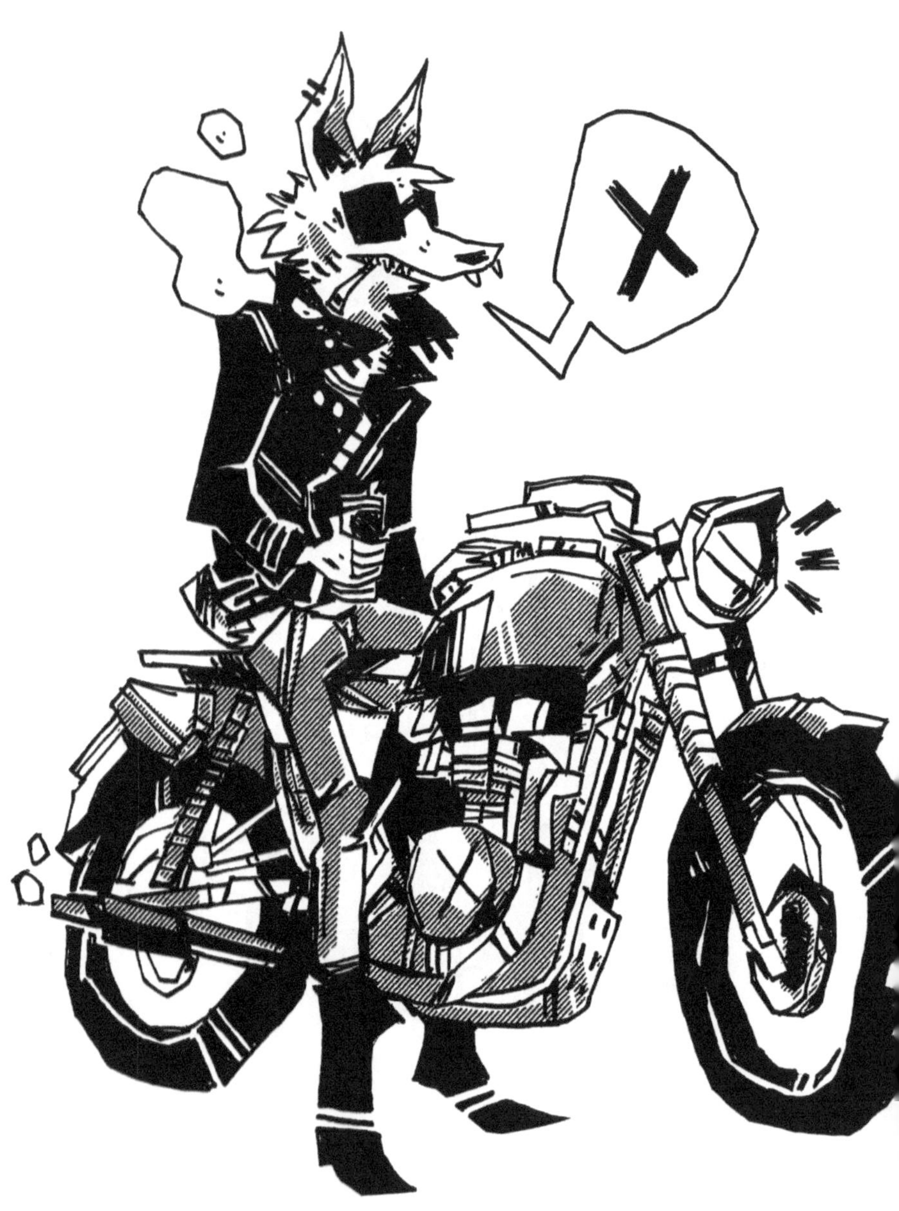

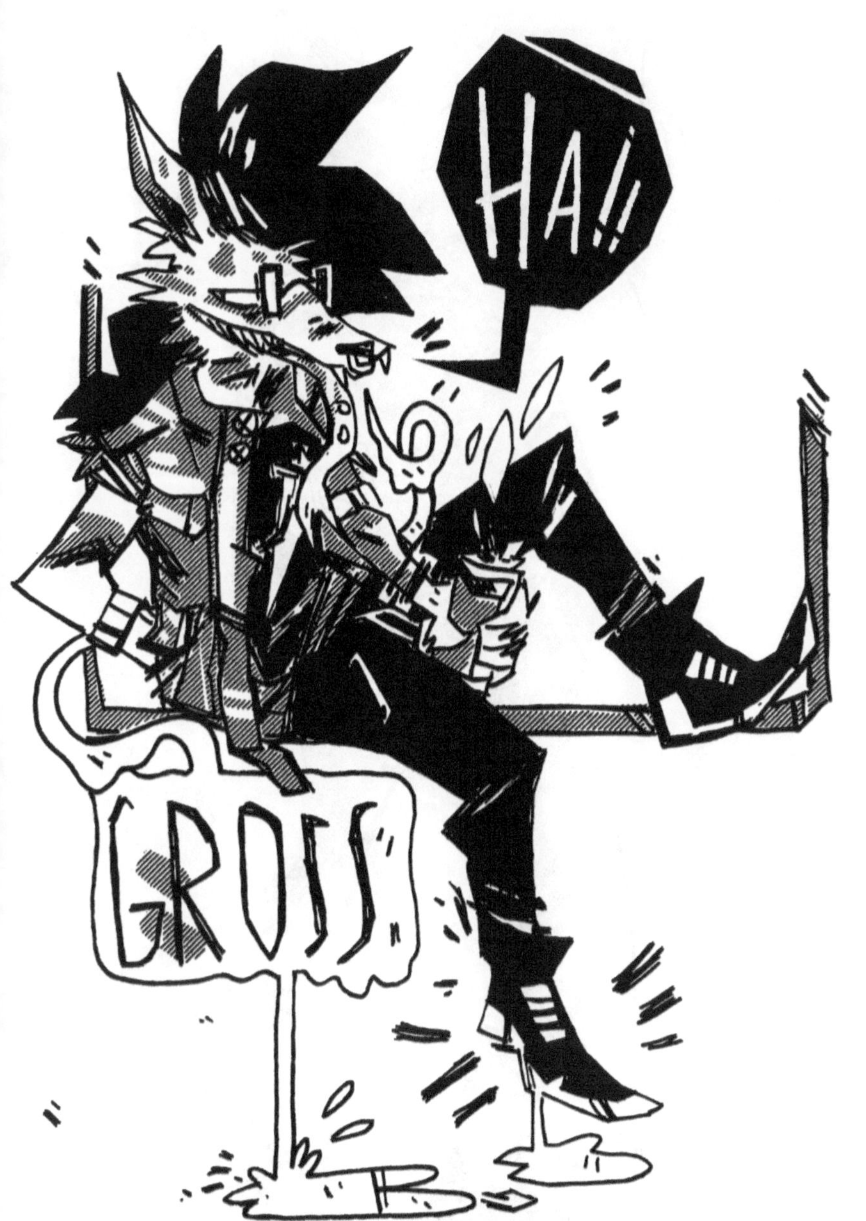

HA!!
GROSS

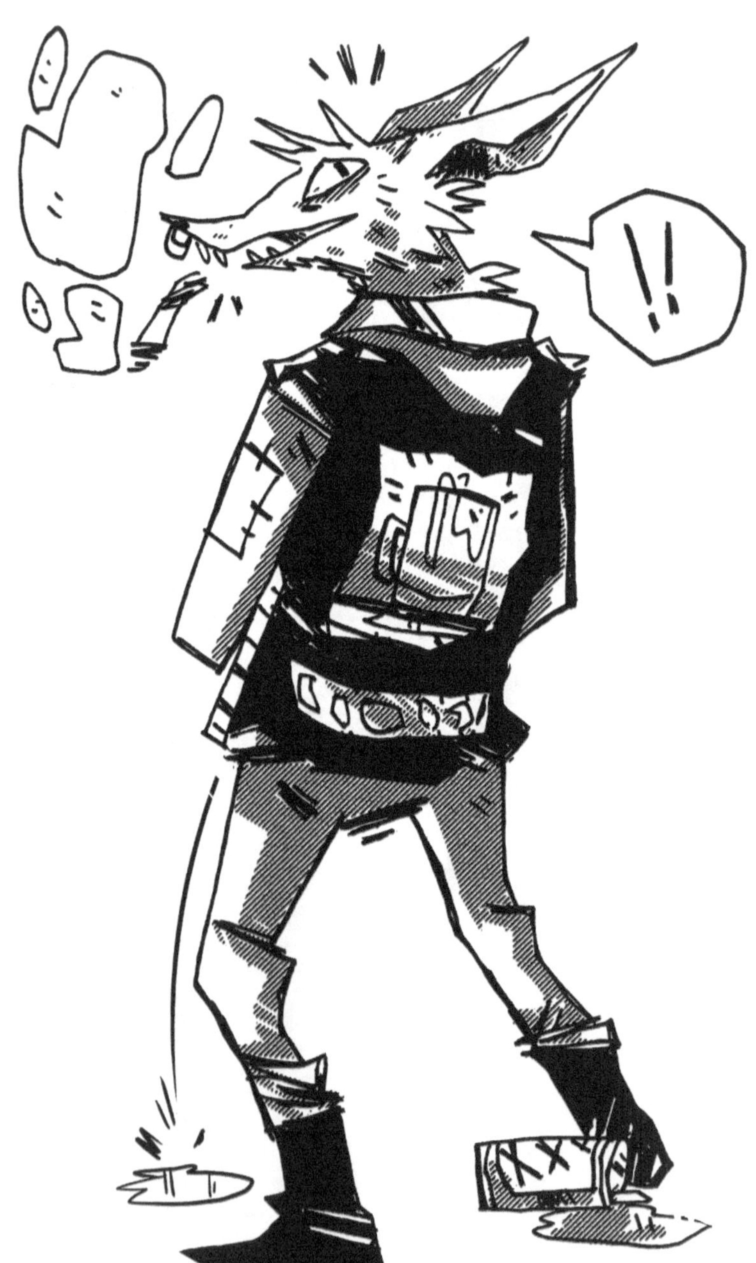

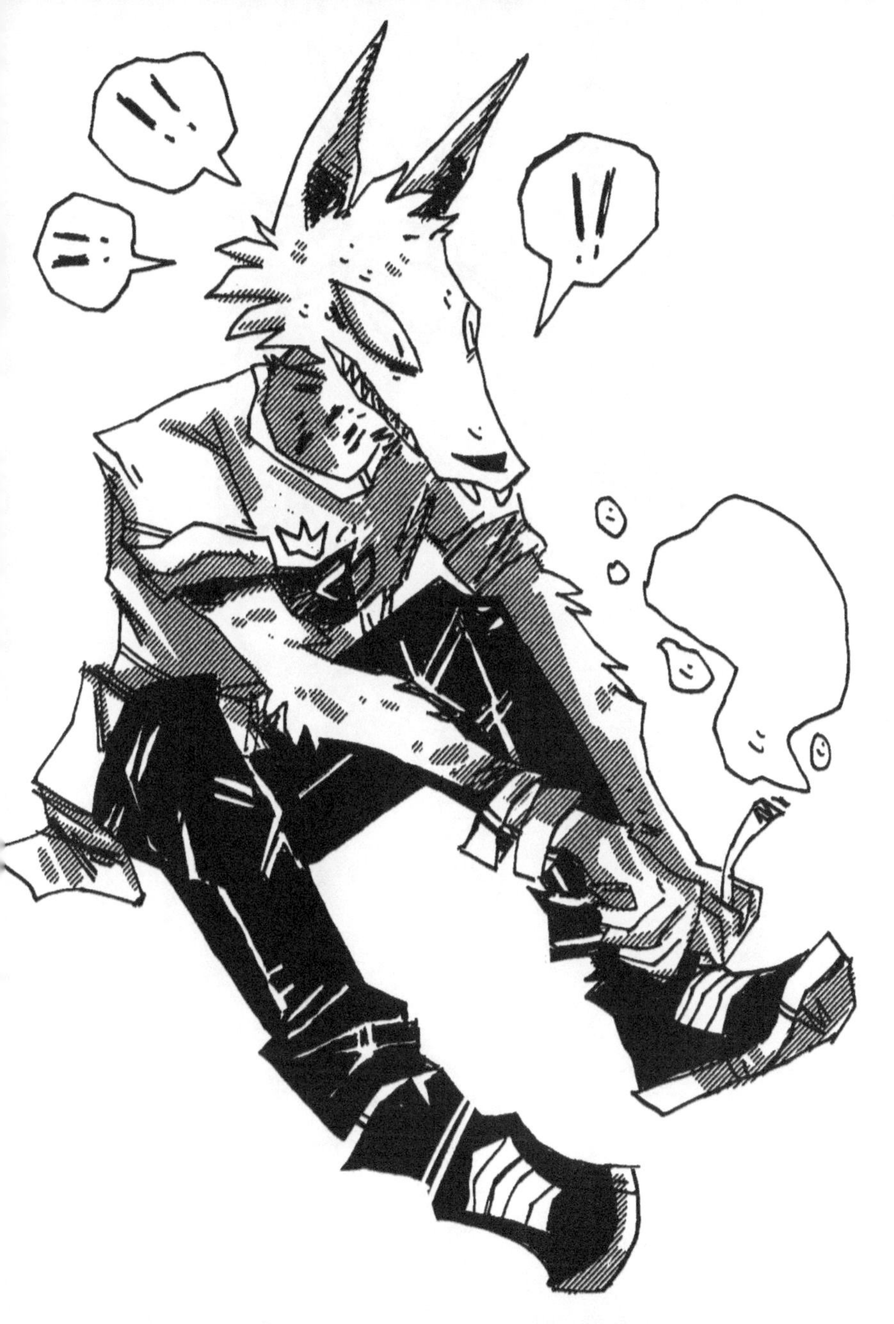

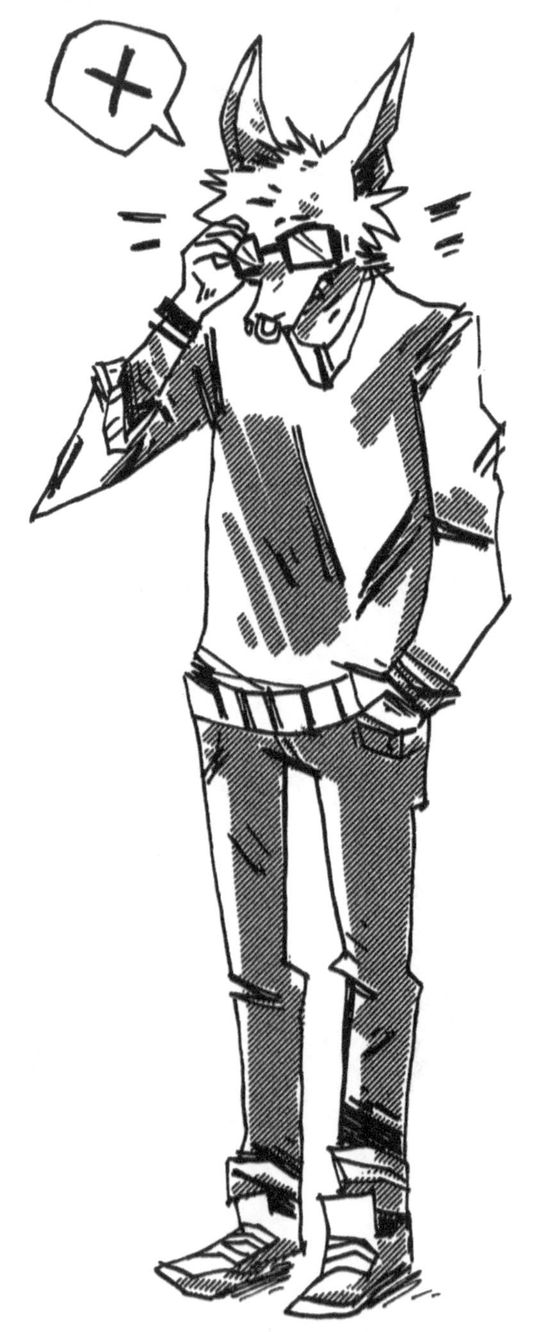

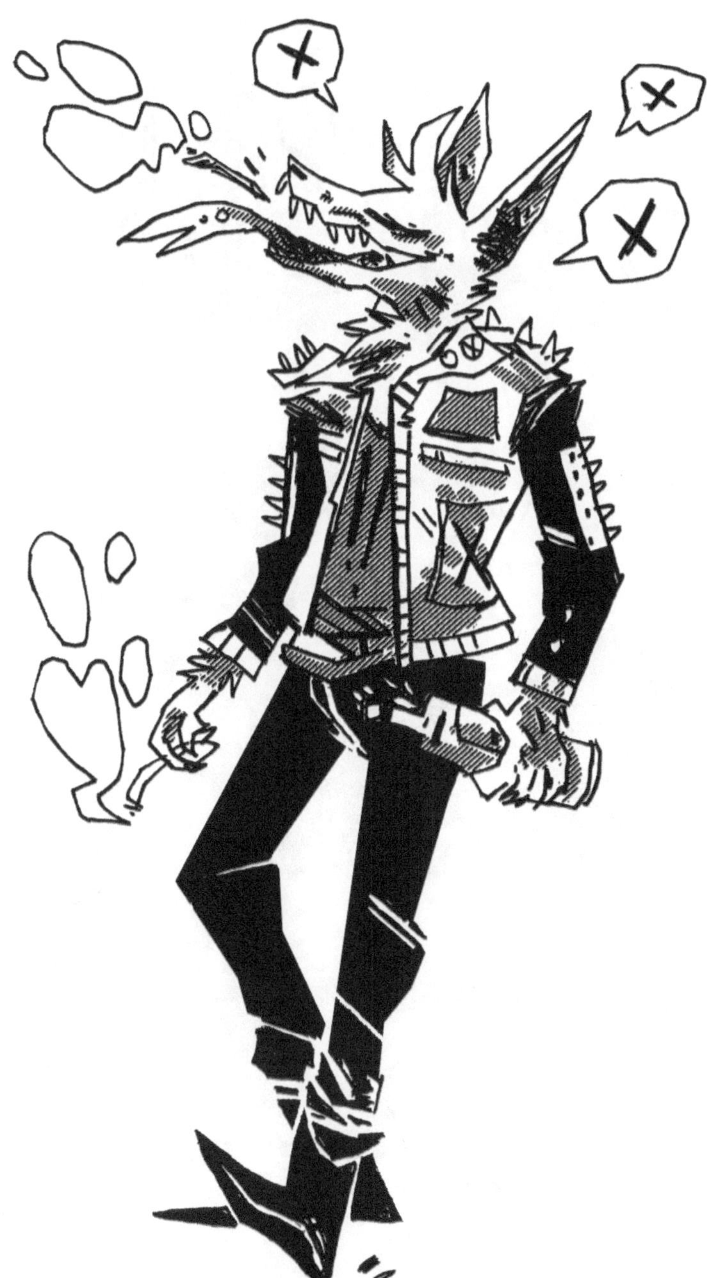
X
X
X

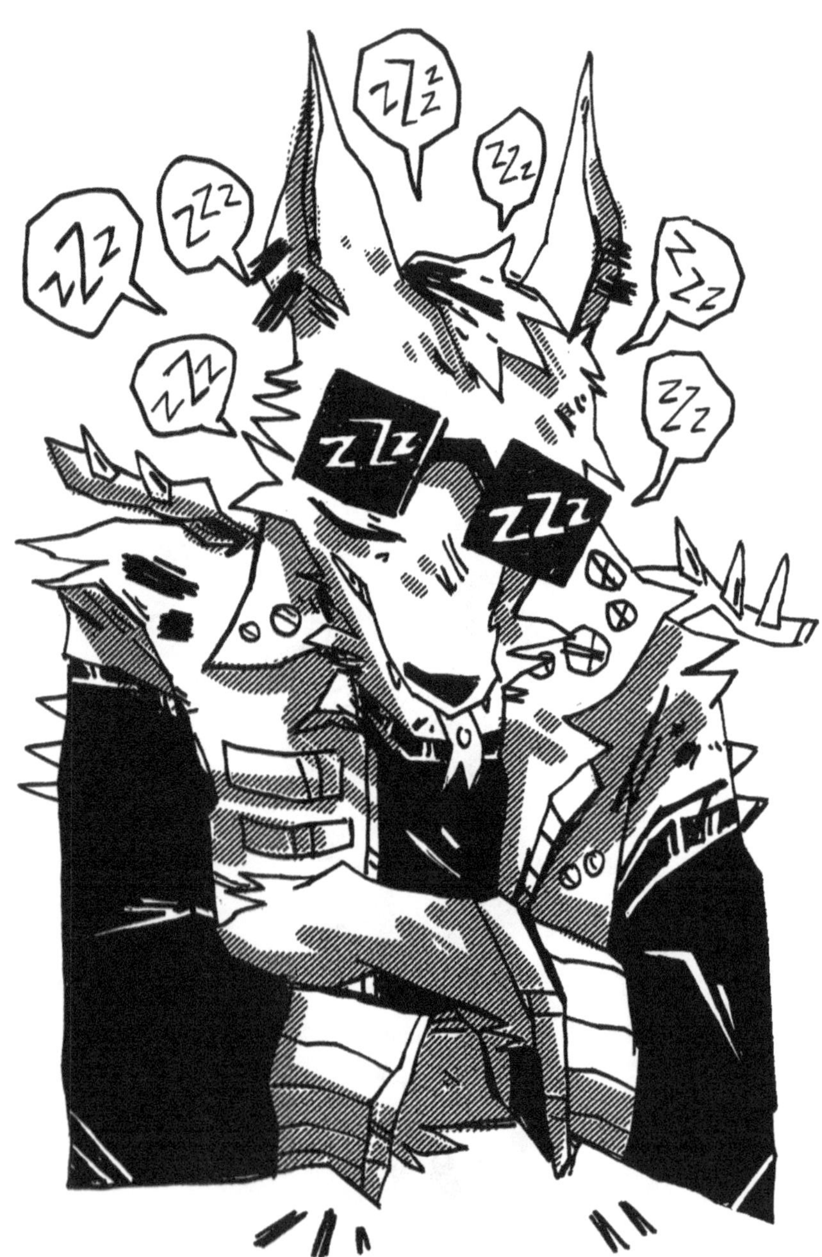

ZZZ
ZZZ
ZZZ
ZZZ
ZZZ
ZZZ
ZZZ
ZZZ
ZZZ

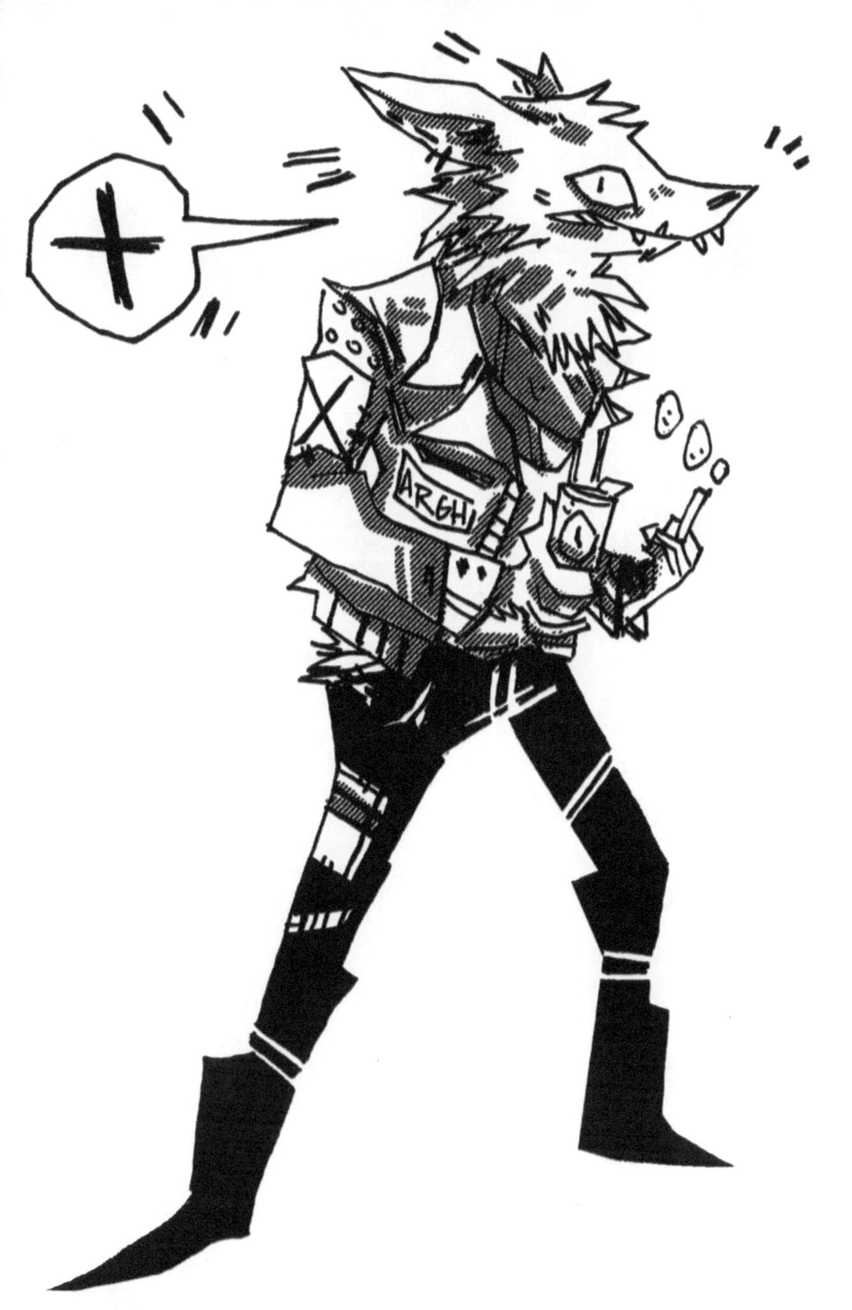
ARGH!

www.ingramcontent.com/pod-product-compliance
Lightning Source LLC
Chambersburg PA
CBHW032135050726
47590CB00008B/3106